Pump it up Magazine

TABLE OF CONTENTS

Letter from The Editor — 5
Anissa Sutton

BISHOP ERNEST JACKSON
Leader in faith for decades. Discover Grace Online Church and find peace in God's name.

TOP TIPS — 11
- How to Stay Mentally Strong
- DIY Holiday Décor for Joy
- Festive Songs to Pump up Your Mood

FASHION
Color Therapy: Pump up your mood!

WELLNESS — 19
Best Superfoods for Energy & Immunity on Christmas

TRAVEL TIPS
Travel in the footstep of Jesus

MUST WATCH — 30
Christmas Movie List!

HUMANITARIAN AWARENESS
The Gift of Giving: How to Help Those in Need This Christmas

FAITH QUIZ
How Strong Is Your Trust in God?

Reach for the Stars – While Standing on Earth!

Pump it up MAGAZINE ®

PUMP IT UP MAGAZINE
LINKS

WEBSITE
www.pumpitupmagazine.com

FACEBOOK
www.facebook.com/pumpitupmagazine

TWITTER
www.twitter.com/pumpitupmag

SOUNDCLOUD
www.soundcloud.com/pumpitupmagazine

INSTAGRAM
pumpitupmagazine

PINTEREST
www.pinterest.com/pumpitupmagazine

PUMP IT UP MAGAZINE
30721 Russell Ranch Road
Suite 140
Westlake Village,
California 91362
United States

 (818)514 – 0038(Ext:102)
 info@pumpitupmagazine.com

LETTER FROM THE EDITOR

Dear Readers,

Merry Christmas and welcome to this super special holiday issue of Pump It Up Magazine! Can you believe the year is almost over? This season always feels like the perfect time to pause, breathe, and soak up all the little joys that make life so beautiful.

This month, we had the privilege of sitting down with Bishop Ernest Jackson, someone whose words truly inspire. His story isn't just about faith—it's about leading with love, finding peace even in tough times, and reminding us of the power of love and kindness. Trust me, his perspective will give you a fresh outlook on what the season is all about.

Our theme, "Pump Up Your Mental Health with Faith & Spirituality This Christmas," is all about taking a step back and giving yourself permission to enjoy the little things. From festive songs to lift your mood to easy DIY holiday décor ideas that bring joy into your home, this issue is like a warm hug in magazine form.

Plus, we've added a fun faith quiz, tips for staying mentally strong, and ideas to help you give back and spread a little extra love this season. And if you're looking for some cozy holiday inspiration, we've got wellness tips, natural snacks, and even a piece on how color therapy can brighten your mood and wardrobe.

So, pour yourself some cocoa, grab your favorite holiday snack, and dive into this edition. Let it inspire you to celebrate the season with joy, kindness, and maybe a few new traditions.

Let's make this Christmas about connection, love, and a whole lot of good vibes.

Wishing you the happiest holiday season!

With love, light, and a little extra sparkle,

Anissa Sutton

Editor-in-Chief
Pump It Up Magazine

CONTRIBUTORS

FOUNDER & EDITOR IN CHIEF
Anissa Boudjaoui Sutton

OWNERS
Anissa & Michael B. Sutton

MARKETING
Grace Rose
Anissa Sutton
Carter Kaya

DESIGN
Afolabi Osho
Anissa Sutton

EDITIONS-LA.COM

PARTNERS

Editions L.A.
www.editions-la.com

The Sound Of L.A.
www.thesoundofla.com

YMC
YourMusicConsultant.com

Info Music
www.infomusic.fr

*P.S. Did you know?
Pump It Up Magazine
is not only online
but also in print and digital,
distributed in more than
100 stores
through print-on-demand.
So, you can catch us
wherever you go!*

GRACE ONLINE CHURCH: TRANSITIONING TO A FULLY ONLINE WORSHIP PLATFORM

Grace Tabernacle Church has transformed into Grace Online Church, a fully digital platform offering worship, faith, and holistic support worldwide. At GraceOnlineChurch.com, access inspiring sermons, live worship, and a supportive faith community—all from the comfort of your home.

"Change creates opportunities to reach more hearts with God's word," shared Bishop Ernest Jackson. "Whether you're a longtime worshiper or new to our family, you're welcome to join this exciting chapter in faith and healing."

What Grace Online Church Offers

Live Streaming Services: Worship live every Sunday at 10:00 AM (PST) on YouTube.

Spotify Podcasts & Playlists: Stay inspired with Christian podcasts and curated worship music.

Interactive Community: Join Bible studies, prayer sessions, and connect globally.

Mental Health Resources: Explore faith-based guidance for emotional well-being.

Monthly Mental Health Support

In partnership with NAMI, Grace Online Church hosts an African American Mental Health Group every second Wednesday of the month. This group offers a safe space to share experiences, find support, and promote healing through faith.

Introducing the Women of Grace

The Women of Grace inspire others through compassion, acts of service, and support for faith and mental health, embodying Grace Online Church's mission.

"Our Women of Grace initiative encourages women to find strength in faith and build supportive communities," said Bishop Ernest Jackson.

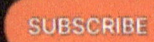

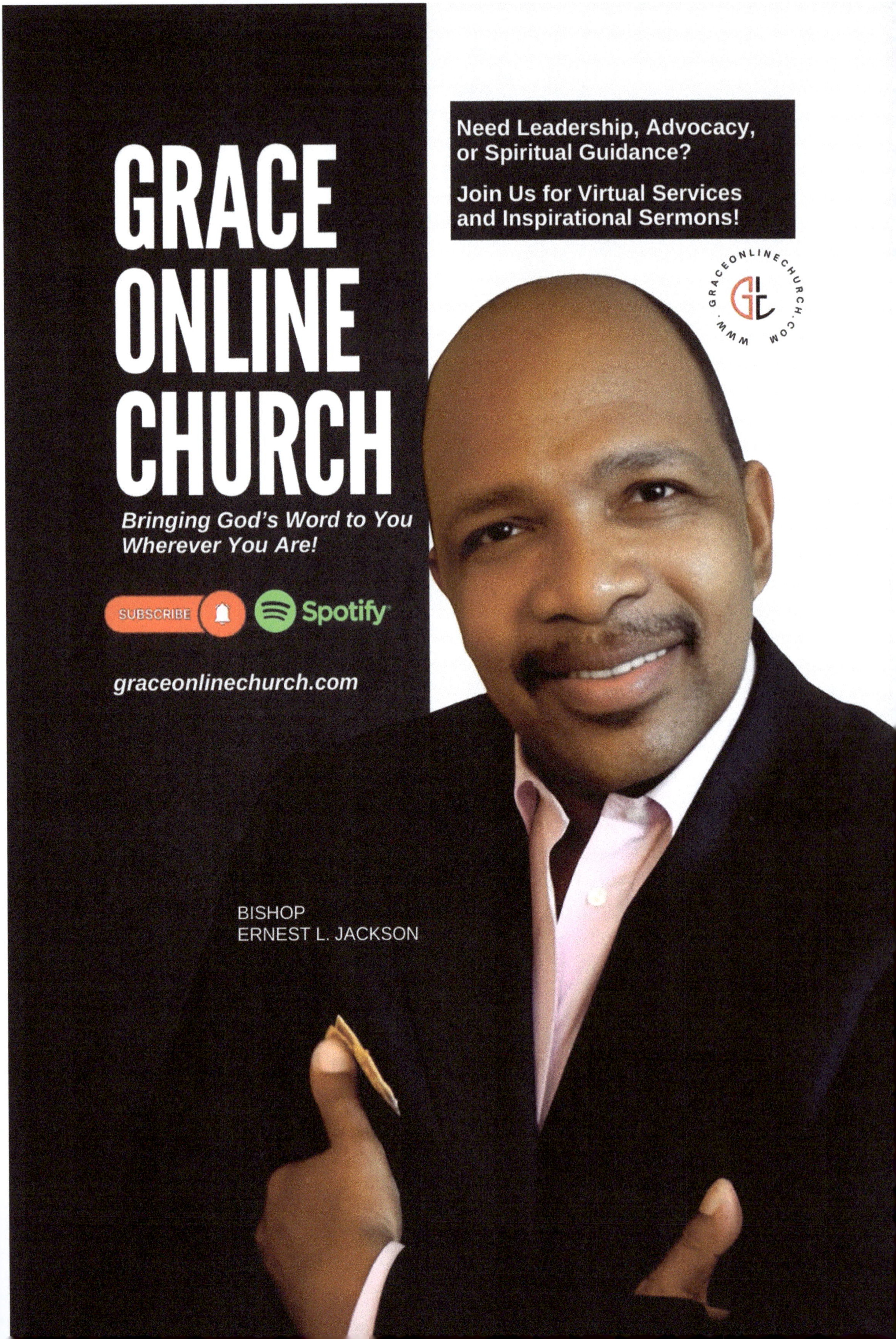
GRACE ONLINE CHURCH
Bringing God's Word to You Wherever You Are!
SUBSCRIBE
Spotify
graceonlinechurch.com
Need Leadership, Advocacy, or Spiritual Guidance?
Join Us for Virtual Services and Inspirational Sermons!
WWW.GRACEONLINECHURCH.COM
BISHOP
ERNEST L. JACKSON

BISHOP ERNEST JACKSON

PIUM: What inspired you to transition Grace Tabernacle Church into Grace Online Church, and how has this shift impacted your congregation?

BISHOP ERNEST JACKSON: The transition of Grace Tabernacle Church into Grace Online Church wasn't something I orchestrated out of personal inspiration or volition—it was an act of obedience to God's will. In truth, I believe I was left without a choice. The shift wasn't about my determination; it was about aligning with God's purpose for this season. Like countless other ministries, during the COVID pandemic, we were called to adapt—not merely for the sake of health compliance, but to embrace God's will for us in this new season. The Holy Spirit reminds us that God's will is evolutionary and if I wanted Grace to prosper and survive, I would have to shift to God's will:

Isaiah 43:18-19 reminds us:
"Forget the former things; do not dwell on the past. See, I am doing a new thing! Now it springs up; do you not perceive it? I am making a way in the wilderness and streams in the wasteland."

PIUM: How does Grace Online Church meet the spiritual needs of worshipers in a digital environment?

BISHOP ERNEST JACKSON: Grace Online Church strives to meet the spiritual needs of worshipers by fostering authentic, global connections that transcend tradition, culture, and religious boundaries. In a digital environment, our mission is to help individuals develop an intimate relationship with God, moving beyond mere knowledge of Him to a transformative faith that anchors their lives with meaning and purpose.

While virtual ministry presents challenges like anonymity and disengagement, it also provides unique opportunities to create an inclusive community centered on shared human experiences and spiritual values. By embracing technology, we unite worshipers from diverse backgrounds, reminding them they are part of something greater—a divine plan that offers hope, purpose, and a future.

Ultimately, Grace Online Church is committed to building meaningful connections, deepening faith, and meeting the universal desire for belonging and spiritual growth in an increasingly digital world.

PIUM: What unique challenges and opportunities have you encountered while leading an online church?

BISHOP ERNEST JACKSON: One of the greatest challenges I've faced in leading an online church has been navigating the transition into a new season—most notably, closing our physical church. This was not just a logistical shift; it was an emotional one, as we grieved the loss of a space that had been a cornerstone of the Bayview Hunters Point community in San Francisco. The impact of COVID-19 was profound, forcing us to adapt to a new way of living and worshiping.

Yet, with change comes opportunity. Recognizing that God is doing a new thing reminds us that while the unknown can be daunting, it also holds untapped possibilities. My hope and confidence lie in trusting God's will and His guidance through this journey.

As Proverbs 3:5-6 teaches: *"Trust in the Lord with all your heart and lean not on your own understanding; in all your ways submit to him, and he will make your paths straight."*

PIUM: Can you share insights about the Men of Grace and your event with NAMI focused on mental health in African American male communities?

BISHOP ERNEST JACKSON: The Men of Grace, in partnership with NAMI, provides a place of comfort where African American men can speak openly and find healing for mental health challenges. Join us every second Wednesday of the month to connect and grow. Details at www.graceonlinechurch.com/events

FIND HEALING THROUGH COMMUNITY WITH OUR BLACK & AFRICAN AMERICAN ALL-MEN SUPPORT GROUP

 **San Francisco**

National Alliance on Mental Illness

Are you tired of wearing an emotional mask and pretending to be okay? Join us in our Black & African American all-men support group as we take our masks off and show up as our true, authentic selves. Led by NAMI-trained volunteers with extensive personal experience coping with mental health challenges, our support group breaks down stigma and fosters a judgment-free zone where we can listen and be heard.

This support group is a safe, confidential space where you can share your experiences and emotions and feel less alone, for others may have gone through similar situations. Together, we can exchange support, provide support, and build hope and understanding. We can learn from each other about local resources, community organizations, and personal coping strategies.

 2nd Wednesday of the Month at 6-7:30 pm

 Virtual - Online via Zoom. Scan the QR Code to register!

Questions - Please call Keesha at (707) 654-3645 or keesha@namisf.org

The National Alliance on Mental Illness (NAMI) is the nation's largest grassroots organization dedicated to improving the lives of individuals living with a mental health condition and their families. At the heart of NAMI San Francisco's mission is sharing information on treatment and recovery and striving to end the stigma associated with mental illness. To this end, we offer a Helpline, support groups, educational classes, and public presentations—at no cost to participants. Visit www.namisf.org for more information

PIUM: How does Grace Online Church address mental health, especially during the holiday season?

BISHOP ERNEST JACKSON: At Grace Online Church, we understand that hopelessness and loneliness can deeply impact the mind, body, and soul, often endured in silence. We believe everyone—especially those facing illness or navigating life alone—deserves to feel seen, valued, and supported. As the holidays approach, we renew our commitment to extending love and compassion, ensuring no one feels forgotten or alone.

Faith in God offers hope, reminding us of our purpose and His divine plan for brighter days. Through prayer, fellowship, and acts of kindness, we create meaningful connections, fostering healing and belonging. At Grace Online Church, love is the bridge that transforms isolation into community and wholeness.

PIUM: What role does your team play in ensuring the success of your ministry and community outreach?

BISHOP ERNEST JACKSON: I emphasize that we are all ministers, each holding a vital piece of the ministry's mission. Unlike the traditional model of church, where the work of evangelizing, teaching, and ministry is left to pastors and leaders, we believe in shared ownership. This collective approach ensures that no one stands on the sidelines. In the virtual church, everyone is called to actively engage, contribute, and lead. This spirit of collaboration not only strengthens our ministry but also fosters growth and deeper community impact. Together, we are the church, united in purpose and action.

PIUM: How can people support Grace Online Church, whether through joining, volunteering, or donations?

BISHOP ERNEST JACKSON: Grace Online Church wants to grow and spread the gospel of Jesus Christ wherever people connect with us. I would love for people to subscribe and follow us through social media. But I want people to contact me via email and even regular mail. Everyone has not adopted to technology; yet, I want still want to hear from them. People can join our community activities, such as this month's Feed 5000, an annual event addressing food insecurity. We join other churches in San Francisco, passing out food to thousands of families who may otherwise go without. We need financial support. You can help us spread the gospel by donating through Givelify, Venmo, Ca$hApp, and PayPal.

PIUM: What message of hope and encouragement would you like to share with those struggling this season?

BISHOP ERNEST JACKSON: I have observed that the world often feels unkind, and many long for peace. When Jesus was born, the angels declared, "Peace on earth, goodwill toward men" (Luke 2:14). This profound message was not merely a wish but a mission for us to embody Christ's love. In a world filled with division and hostility, we are called to reflect His peace and kindness in every interaction.

Stevie Wonder's "Love is in Need of Love" resonates with this truth. Though secular, it speaks to the universal power of love as the antidote to hate and despair. Both the angels' proclamation and this song remind us of our role in spreading compassion and understanding.

As followers of Christ, we are agents of change, tasked with bringing the light of His love into dark places. Simple acts—listening without judgment, helping those in need, and showing kindness—allow God's peace to flow through us. These actions demonstrate that everyone is valued, loved, and worthy of grace.

My message would be this: Let Christ's love transform your heart. Allow it to inspire compassion and understanding in your daily life. When we embody His love, we fulfill the angels' call for "peace on earth, goodwill toward men," becoming living examples of His peace and showing the world that love is still the answer.

Mental Health Tips

HOW TO STAY MENTALLY STRONG

Life's challenges can sometimes feel overwhelming, but building mental strength helps you navigate them with resilience and confidence. Here are practical tips to stay mentally strong and maintain a positive outlook.

1. PRACTICE SELF-COMPASSION
Treat yourself with kindness and understanding, especially during difficult times. Replace self-criticism with encouragement, and remember, everyone makes mistakes.

2. FOCUS ON WHAT YOU CAN CONTROL
Shift your energy to areas where you have influence rather than dwelling on uncontrollable circumstances. This helps you stay proactive and reduces stress.

3. DEVELOP HEALTHY HABITS
Engage in regular exercise, eat nourishing foods, and prioritize sleep. Physical well-being is closely tied to mental health.

4. BUILD A SUPPORT NETWORK
Surround yourself with positive and supportive people. Share your thoughts with trusted friends or family, or consider joining a support group.

5. SET REALISTIC GOALS
Break big goals into smaller, manageable steps. Celebrate your achievements, no matter how small, to build momentum and confidence.

6. PRACTICE GRATITUDE
Take time each day to reflect on things you're grateful for. Gratitude shifts your focus to the positive aspects of life and boosts resilience.

7. EMBRACE MINDFULNESS
Incorporate mindfulness or meditation into your daily routine to stay present and reduce anxiety. Even a few minutes of deep breathing can have a calming effect.

8. LEARN FROM SETBACKS
View failures as opportunities to grow. Reflect on what you can learn from challenges, and use those lessons to move forward stronger than before.

9. LIMIT NEGATIVE INPUTS
Reduce exposure to negative news or toxic environments. Protecting your mental space is essential for maintaining strength and focus.

9. LIMIT NEGATIVE INPUTS
There's no shame in seeking guidance from a therapist , or religious counselor. Professional support can provide valuable tools to strengthen your mental resilience.

Editions L.A.

DIGITAL CREATIVE AGENCY

We Transform Your Vision Into Creative Results

Editions L.A. is a full-service agency based in Los Angeles. Our company is a collective of amazing people striving to build delightful services
We believe that is all about getting your message across clearly and with a "Wow!" thrown in for good measure.

Our Awesome Services

Branding

We build, style and tone your brand identity from the ground up.
We rebrand established bands, brands or businesses.

Merchandise Store
Website design and E-Commerce
Website updates

Digital Marketing

CD Cover | Banners | Logo design | Flyers | Brochures |
Leaflets | Print ads | Magazine covers & artworks
Facebook / twitter / instagram / youtube artworks
| Book cover
Infographics | Icon Design |
| TshirtsProduct Labels | Presentation slides
Corporate graphics
Professional photo editing & enhancing
Redesign existing elements
YouTube Optimization and Monetization
Youtube Video Editing
Lyric Video and Advertising Design.

Publishing

BOOK COVER DESIGN
EBOOK FORMATTING SERVICES
and distribution on major platforms
(Amazon, Barnes & Nobles..)

Tell us about your dream and we will make it true!

Editions L.A.
7210 Jordan Avenue Suite B42, Canoga Park, California 91303, United States
info@edtions-la.com
Website: www.editions-la.com

Christmas Gifts Ideas!

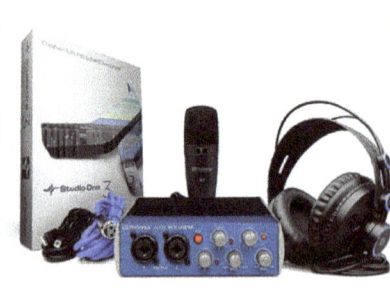

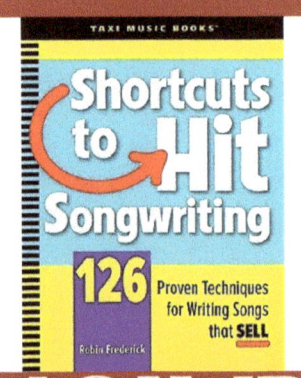

FOR SONGWRITERS & MUSICIANS

Your loved ones deserve a gift just as unique as their passion.

Christmas Tips

DIY HOLIDAY DÉCOR FOR JOY

Bring joy to your home this holiday season with creative and budget-friendly DIY décor ideas. These projects are fun, festive, and sure to fill your space with holiday cheer.

1. HANDMADE WREATHS
Use natural elements like pinecones, evergreen branches, and berries to craft a beautiful holiday wreath. Add a personal touch with ribbons or ornaments.

2. MASON JAR LUMINARIES
Fill mason jars with fairy lights, pine sprigs, or small ornaments for a cozy glow. You can also use frosted spray paint for a wintry effect.

3. FESTIVE GARLANDS
String together dried orange slices, cinnamon sticks, and cranberries for a rustic garland. Drape it over your mantel or around a doorway for a warm, festive vibe.

4. ORNAMENT CENTERPIECES
Gather your unused ornaments and place them in a decorative bowl or glass vase. Add tinsel or string lights for extra sparkle.

5. PERSONALIZED STOCKINGS
Decorate plain stockings with fabric paint, glitter, or iron-on patches. Add names or unique designs to make them special for each family member.

6. DIY ADVENT CALENDAR
Create an advent calendar using small envelopes, bags, or boxes. Fill each with treats, notes, or small trinkets to count down the days until Christmas.

7. SNOWFLAKE WINDOW CLINGS
Cut snowflake designs out of white paper or use craft foam. Stick them to your windows for a whimsical, wintry look.

8. UPCYCLED CANDLE HOLDERS
Repurpose old jars or cans by wrapping them in burlap, ribbon, or twine. Add a tea light inside for a charming holiday accent.

9. HOLIDAY PILLOW COVERS
Transform your living room with festive pillow covers. Use stencils and fabric paint to create seasonal designs on plain covers.

10. DIY TREE ORNAMENTS
Make your own ornaments using salt dough, clay, or felt.
Let your creativity shine by painting or embellishing them with glitter and beads.
Add some holiday music and scents like cinnamon or peppermint to complete the festive atmosphere.
These DIY projects will not only beautify your home but also create lasting memories with loved ones.
Happy decorating!

HAPPY HOLIDAYS!
CHRISTMAS SONGS

This selection is sure to fill your heart with the joy of Christmas!

Anessa — Santa Baby

Victoria Renée — Oh Holy Night
A Timeless Christmas Classic

Ashley Gronholm — Miracle in Me

Cindy Davis — Wait On You

WWW.PUMPITUPMAGAZINE.COM/RADIO

Fashion Tips — 16-34

Photo by Snack Toronto: https://www.pexels.com/photo/yellow-steel-bathtub-1630344

COLOR THERAPY: PUMP UP YOUR MOOD!

Colors are more than just a feast for the eyes; they carry profound energy that can impact your emotions, well-being, and even your spiritual state. From a holistic perspective, the colors you choose to surround yourself with—whether in your wardrobe or environment—can align your energy, elevate your mood, and bring balance to your life. Let's explore how the energy of color can be harnessed to create harmony and positivity.

RED: THE ENERGY OF VITALITY AND PASSION
Red is a powerful color associated with the root chakra, symbolizing vitality, stability, and passion. Wearing red can boost your physical energy, increase your confidence, and stimulate motivation. It's a great choice for moments when you need courage or a sense of grounding.

YELLOW: THE ENERGY OF JOY AND OPTIMISM
Yellow resonates with the solar plexus chakra, which governs personal power and happiness. This bright and cheerful hue can uplift your mood, enhance mental clarity, and spark creativity. Incorporate yellow into your life on days when you need an emotional pick-me-up.

BLUE: THE ENERGY OF CALM AND COMMUNICATION
Blue aligns with the throat chakra, representing clarity, communication, and tranquility. Light blue shades promote relaxation and peace, while deeper blues can encourage introspection and thoughtful communication. Use blue to balance emotions and improve focus.

GREEN: THE ENERGY OF BALANCE AND RENEWAL
Green is connected to the heart chakra, symbolizing love, balance, and harmony. It fosters feelings of renewal and connection to nature. Adding green to your wardrobe or space can help you feel centered and at peace with yourself and others.

PINK: THE ENERGY OF COMPASSION AND LOVE
Pink combines the passion of red and the purity of white, embodying unconditional love and compassion. It aligns with the higher heart chakra, promoting self-love and kindness. Soft pinks bring soothing energy, while brighter pinks add vibrancy and playfulness.

PURPLE: THE ENERGY OF SPIRITUAL AWARENESS
Purple is associated with the crown chakra, symbolizing spiritual connection, wisdom, and creativity. Wearing purple or surrounding yourself with this color can inspire deeper thought, meditation, and a sense of luxury or inner peace.

ORANGE: THE ENERGY OF CREATIVITY AND JOY
Orange resonates with the sacral chakra, linked to creativity, joy, and emotional expression. It's a warm and invigorating color that can spark enthusiasm and help release blocked emotions. Incorporate orange when you need a boost of inspiration.

Funk Therapy

| Funky | Trendy | Cool | Hip |

Wear The Music You Love!

Visit our merchandise store on our website:

WWW.FUNKTHERAPYMUSIC.COM

10% Discount code: STAYFUNKY

- Hoodies
- Crop Top
- Sweat Pants
- Bucket Hats
- Slides
- Mugs

UNISEX T-SHIRTS

Brown T-Shirt

GRAB IT NOW

Orange T-Shirt

GRAB IT NOW

Beige T-Shirts

GRAB IT NOW

Join our community
@funktherapy2

Wellness Tips

BEST SUPERFOODS FOR ENERGY & IMMUNITY ON CHRISTMAS

The holiday season is filled with indulgent treats, but incorporating superfoods into your diet can keep your energy up and your immunity strong. Here are the best superfoods to keep you feeling your best this Christmas:

1. CITRUS FRUITS
Oranges, grapefruits, and lemons are rich in vitamin C, which boosts immunity and helps ward off seasonal colds. Add them to salads, desserts, or enjoy as fresh juice.

2. GINGER
Known for its anti-inflammatory and digestive benefits, ginger is perfect for soothing holiday indulgences. Use it in teas, cookies, or festive dishes.

3. NUTS AND SEEDS
Almonds, walnuts, chia seeds, and flaxseeds are packed with healthy fats, protein, and fiber to provide sustained energy throughout the day. They also make great additions to baked goods and salads.

4. DARK LEAFY GREENS
Kale, spinach, and Swiss chard are loaded with vitamins and antioxidants. Include them in soups, side dishes, or even holiday smoothies to stay energized.

5. BERRIES
Blueberries, cranberries, and goji berries are antioxidant powerhouses. They boost immunity and can be used in desserts, oatmeal, or as festive garnishes.

6. SWEET POTATOES
A great source of complex carbohydrates and vitamin A, sweet potatoes provide steady energy and support overall health. Roast them with cinnamon for a holiday twist.

7. HONEY
A natural sweetener with antimicrobial properties, honey is great for soothing sore throats and boosting energy. Drizzle it on yogurt, toast, or holiday treats.

8. TURMERIC
This golden spice is known for its immune-boosting and anti-inflammatory properties. Add it to teas, soups, or roasted vegetables for a flavorful health kick.

9. DARK CHOCOLATE
Rich in antioxidants and a natural mood booster, dark chocolate is a festive treat that supports heart health and provides a quick energy boost. Choose options with at least 70% cocoa.

10. GREEN TEA
Packed with antioxidants and a gentle caffeine boost, green tea is perfect for staying alert and supporting immunity during the holiday rush.

FINAL TIPS

Balance indulgence with these superfoods to enjoy a healthier and more energized Christmas. Whether added to meals or enjoyed as snacks, these nutrient-packed options will help you thrive through the festive season.

EXPLORE
The World

WHY YOU SHOULD CONSIDER TRAVELING IN A MOTOR HOME

Freedom

When you travel with a motor home, you have the ultimate freedom to explore the world. You can go wherever you want, when you want and stay as long as you desire. No need to worry about finding a place to stay, looking for public transportation or dealing with airline tickets!

Affordability

You'll save money on accommodation since you'll be staying in your own self-contained living space. You'll also save money on food costs since you'll have a fully functioning kitchen in your motor home. Not to mention, you'll save money on transport as your motor home will get you from point A to point B.

Comfort

You will have access to a full kitchen, living area, sleeping quarters and bathroom, all in one vehicle. This means that you won't have to worry about packing up your things each time you move from one place to another. Plus, you don't have to worry about expensive hotel bills when you stay on the road for long periods of time.

BOOK NOW

- 123981 Craftsman Rd., Calabasas, CA 91302
- 1(818) 225-8239
- www.expeditionmotorhomes.com/

TRAVEL IN THE FOOTSTEPS OF JESUS: A SPIRITUAL JOURNEY THROUGH THE HOLY LAND

1. NAZARETH
Start in Nazareth, Jesus's childhood home. Visit the Basilica of the Annunciation, believed to be where the Angel Gabriel appeared to Mary, and explore nearby Nazareth Village, a recreation of a 1st-century village

2. SEA OF GALILEE
Head to the Sea of Galilee, where Jesus performed many miracles. Take a boat ride on the tranquil waters and visit Capernaum, known as "Jesus's own city."

3. MOUNT OF BEATITUDES
Reflect on Jesus's teachings at the Mount of Beatitudes, where He delivered the Sermon on the Mount. It offers a peaceful setting for prayer and meditation.

4. JORDAN RIVER
Experience a moment of renewal at the Jordan River, where Jesus was baptized by John the Baptist. Some sites offer the opportunity for visitors to renew their baptismal vows.

5. JERUSALEM
In Jerusalem, visit the Garden of Gethsemane, the Via Dolorosa, and the Church of the Holy Sepulchre, the site of Jesus's crucifixion and resurrection.

6. BETHLEHEM
Visit Bethlehem, the birthplace of Jesus. The Church of the Nativity marks the site of His birth, featuring a serene grotto that attracts pilgrims worldwide.

7. MOUNT TABOR
Experience the Mount of Transfiguration, where Jesus was transformed before Peter, James, and John. The panoramic views and Church of the Transfiguration make this a spiritually uplifting stop.

8. DEAD SEA
Take a detour to the Dead Sea, famous for its mineral-rich waters. While not directly tied to Jesus, it offers a place for relaxation and reflection.

9. BETHANY
Visit Bethany, home to Mary, Martha, and Lazarus. See the Tomb of Lazarus, where Jesus raised him from the dead, symbolizing hope and renewal.

10. QUMRAN CAVES
Explore the Qumran Caves, where the Dead Sea Scrolls were discovered. This site offers insights into Jewish history and biblical texts from Jesus's time.

11. MOUNT OF OLIVES
The Mount of Olives offers panoramic views of Jerusalem and is significant for Jesus's teachings and His ascension into heaven.

12. EIN KAREM
Explore Ein Karem, believed to be the birthplace of John the Baptist, and visit the Church of the Visitation, where Mary met Elizabeth.

I AM - JE SUIS

AFFIRMATIONS POUR LA PENSÉE POSITIVE
AFFIRMATIONS FOR POSITIVE THINKING

Color & Learn French with Every Page!

Benefits

- **Bilingual Skills:** Get a head start on French and English.
- **Positive Thinking:** Helps kids see the bright side.
- **Confidence Boost:** Full of confidence-building affirmations.
- **Fun Learning:** Who knew coloring could teach you a language?
- **Creativity Kick:** Boosts those creative and motor skills.
- **Smarter Every Day:** Sharpens memory and helps kids multitask.
- **Worldly Wise:** Opens up a world of cultures.
- **Family Time:** Perfect for some fun learning together.
- **Invest in the Future:** Sets kids up for success down the road.

WWW.BILINGUALBOOKSTORE.COM

Wellness

HOW TO SAY NO!
Protecting Yourself and Feeling Confident

Saying 'No' isn't just a refusal; it's a potent tool for maintaining balance, setting boundaries, and safeguarding your mental health. Frequently underestimated, the ability to say 'No' is vital across different life facets, from effectively managing personal time to nurturing healthier relationships. Exploring the significance of saying 'No,' let's delve into ten compelling reasons why mastering this skill matters and discover actionable tips for executing it with effectiveness

I. PRESERVING YOUR TIME AND ENERGY:
Prioritize commitments and assess alignment with your priorities before agreeing. Politely decline by stating, *"I'd love to help, but I'm currently committed elsewhere."*

II. ESTABLISHING BOUNDARIES:
Communicate your limits directly yet respectfully. For instance, *"I appreciate your offer, but I'm unable to take on extra tasks right now."*

III. PROTECTING YOUR MENTAL HEALTH:
Understand that saying "No" isn't selfish; it's a form of self-care. Kindly decline if something doesn't contribute positively to your well-being, saying, *"I need to take care of myself right now."*

IV. EMPOWERING PERSONAL GROWTH:
Evaluate opportunities before committing. Decline distractions to allow experiences fostering personal and professional growth.

V. STRENGTHENING RELATIONSHIPS:
Be honest and gracious in your declines. Express appreciation while declining politely, such as, *"I'm honored, but I'm unable to participate at this time."*

VI. ENHANCING DECISION-MAKING:
Pause before agreeing impulsively. Consider your commitments and use language like, *"Let me check my schedule and get back to you."*

VII. DEVELOPING ASSERTIVENESS:
Practice saying "No" gradually. Use positive language such as, *"I need to focus on my priorities right now."*

VIII. ENCOURAGING SELF-CARE:
Prioritize yourself without guilt. Emphasize the importance of self-care by saying, *"I've scheduled personal time that I can't change."*

IX. LEARNING TO PRIORITIZE:
Recognize your limits and the urgency of requests. Decline politely by stating, *"It doesn't align with my priorities."*

X. SAYING 'NO' WITHIN FAMILY OR PARENTAL CONTEXTS:
Respectfully decline within family or parental contexts, ensuring clear communication and understanding of your boundaries. Express gratitude and understanding while politely declining, such as, *"I appreciate your request, but at the moment, I'm unable to accommodate."*

X!. EFFECTIVE COMMUNICATION:
Use direct yet polite language. Offer a brief explanation if necessary, without over-explaining. Be assertive yet kind: *"I'm sorry, I'm fully booked at the moment"*

For more helpful tips, visit www.pumpitupmagazine.com/wellness

Wellness

HOW TO HEAL WITH BINAURAL BEATS & SOLFEGGIOS FREQUENCIES

Ancient melodies hold the secrets of well-being, and within Solfeggio Frequencies' harmonies lies transformative healing. Let's explore each note's unique resonance and its contributions to our health.

BINAURAL BEATS:

Alpha Waves 8–12 Hz Relaxation, creativity, stress reduction, calm focus
Beta Waves 14–40 Hz Increased concentration, alertness, enhanced cognitive performance
Theta Waves 4–8 Hz Deep relaxation, meditation, access to the subconscious mind
Delta Waves 0.5–4 Hz Deep sleep, healing, restoration, regeneration

SOLFEGGIOS FREQUENCIES

I. 174 Hz - The Foundation of Healing: Effects on pain relief, tension reduction, stress alleviation, and its connection to physical healing, establishing the groundwork for wellness.

II. 285 HZ - Restoring Energy and Balance: Its influence on tissue healing, immune enhancement, root chakra balance, and its role in restoring emotional equilibrium.

III. 396 HZ - Liberating from Fear and Guilt: This frequency aids in releasing fear-based thinking, transforming grief, and facilitating emotional healing.

IV. 417 HZ - Releasing Negativity and Emotional Healing: Potential to dispel negativity, aid trauma recovery, restore emotional equilibrium, and promote restful sleep.

V. 432 HZ - Resonance with Natural Harmony: Alignment with Earth's frequency, anxiety reduction, DNA repair, and fostering creativity.

VI. 528 HZ - The Love Frequency: Reputation for nurturing love, fostering positivity, DNA repair, and enhancing creative inspiration.

VII. 639 HZ - Harmonizing Relationships: Potential to mend relationships, enhance emotional expression, and foster forgiveness.

VIII. 741 HZ - Expressing Authenticity: Role in detoxification, authentic emotional expression, dispelling lies, and aiding in truth-seeking.

IX. 852 HZ - Awakening Intuition: Impact on intuition, spiritual awareness, and role in self-understanding and personal growth.

X. 963 HZ - Transcending Consciousness: Association with higher consciousness, cosmic connection, and accessing divine knowledge.

Solfeggio Frequencies offer a path to holistic healing. For an enhanced experience, use headphones or earphones while exploring these therapeutic tones on platforms like YouTube or streaming services. Embrace the potential benefits for personal well-being and inner harmony.
Wishing you peace, vitality, and a melody-filled path to holistic health! For more insights, visit www.westendorganix.com and embark on your journey towards inner balance and well-being!

GLOBAL FREQUENCY
EVERYDAY 5PM (PST)
KPIU RADIO

LISTEN TO GLOBAL FREQUENCY EVERYDAY

HIP HOP - R&B - EDM

5PM - 6PM (PST) ON WWW.KPIURADIO.COM

HIP HOP - R&B - EDM HOSTED BY GRANDMIXER GMS

KPIURADIO.COM

@KPIURADIO
@PUMPITUPMAGAZINE

SONG REQUEST
KPIURADIO.COM/DEDICACES-1

WWW.KPIURADIO.COM

MUST WATCH

CHRISTMAS

MOVIES

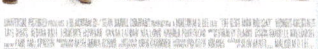

Pump it up magazine

Reach for the stars, while standing on earth!

THE GIFT OF GIVING
The holiday season is a time of joy and celebration, but for many, it can also be a time of struggle. This Christmas, consider embracing the spirit of giving by helping those in need. Here are some meaningful ways to make a difference:

1. DONATE TO LOCAL CHARITIES
Consider giving to organizations like GraceOnlineChurch.com, which supports communities in need with mental health, wellness, food, clothing, and resources.
Support organizations that provide food, clothing, and shelter to those in need. Whether it's a monetary donation or gently used items, every contribution counts.

2. VOLUNTEER YOUR TIME
Many shelters and food banks need extra hands during the holiday season. Volunteering your time can bring relief and joy to those who rely on these services.

3. CREATE CARE PACKAGES
Assemble care packages with essentials like toiletries, non-perishable snacks, and warm clothing. Distribute them to homeless individuals or donate them to shelters.

4. SUPPORT FAMILIES IN CRISIS
Reach out to local organizations that assist families facing hardships. Consider adopting a family for the holidays by providing gifts, groceries, or paying a utility bill.

5. HOST A FUNDRAISER
Organize a holiday bake sale, charity run, or virtual fundraiser to raise money for a cause close to your heart. Engage your community to amplify the impact.

6. SHARE A MEAL
Invite someone who might be alone this holiday season to join your family dinner. Sharing a meal can provide comfort and connection.

7. OFFER YOUR SKILLS
If you have a special skill, such as cooking, tutoring, or crafting, consider offering it to those in need. Free services can brighten someone's day.

8. SPREAD KINDNESS
Small acts of kindness, like writing holiday cards for seniors or paying for someone's coffee, can create a ripple effect of positivity.

FINAL THOUGHTS

The true gift of Christmas is the joy of giving. By reaching out to those in need, you not only brighten their holiday season but also enrich your own with the warmth of compassion.
Let's make this Christmas a season of kindness and generosity.

HOW STRONG IS YOUR TRUST IN GOD? FAITH QUIZ

1. When faced with uncertainty, how do you respond?
a) I pray and trust that God will guide me. (3 points)
b) I worry but eventually remind myself to trust in God. (2 points)
c) I often rely on my own understanding and rarely turn to prayer. (1 point)

2. How often do you spend time in prayer or devotion?
a) Daily, it's a key part of my routine. (3 points)
b) Occasionally, when I feel the need. (2 points)
c) Rarely or only in times of crisis. (1 point)

3. When things don't go as planned, what's your mindset?
a) I trust God has a bigger plan and remain hopeful. (3 points)
b) I feel frustrated but try to keep faith. (2 points)
c) I feel defeated and struggle to find purpose in it. (1 point)

4. When faced with a stressful situation, how do you react?
A) I panic and feel overwhelmed
B) I take a few deep breaths and try to stay calm
C) I focus on solutions and maintain control

4. How do you approach decisions in your life?
a) I seek God's guidance and wisdom through prayer. (3 points)
b) I try to make the best decision but sometimes forget to pray. (2 points)
c) I make decisions on my own without seeking God's input. (1 point)

5. How often do you feel God's presence in your life?
a) Frequently, I feel His presence daily. (3 points)
b) Occasionally, during worship or in meaningful moments. (2 points)
c) Rarely, I struggle to feel connected. (1 point)

SCORING YOUR RESULTS

Score 12-15: Unshakeable Faith

Your trust in God is strong and deeply rooted. You consistently turn to Him for guidance and feel His presence in your life. Keep nurturing your faith through prayer and devotion, and continue to be a light to those around you.

Score 8-11: Growing Faith

Your faith is solid, but there's room for growth. You trust God in many areas of your life but may sometimes falter. Strengthen your relationship through regular prayer, reflection, and seeking His wisdom in all situations.

Score 5-7: Faith Under Construction:

You're on a journey to build trust in God. While you may struggle to fully rely on Him, this is an opportunity to deepen your faith. Spend more time in prayer and Scripture to develop a closer relationship with God.

Take time to reflect on your results and seek ways to grow closer to God. Remember, faith is a journey, and every step you take brings you closer to Him.

The 5-Days Love *Yourself Challenge*

Day 01 — Write Down What You Love About You

Day 02 — Create A Happiness Playlist

Day 03 — Cook Yourself A Nice Meal

Day 04 — Practice Self-Affirmation

Day 05 — Approach Your Problem With Mindfulness

@pumpitupmagazine

How anxious are you?

OVER THE LAST 2 WEEKS, HOW OFTEN HAVE YOU BEEN BOTHERED BY THE FOLLOWING PROBLEMS	Not at all	Several days	More than half the days	Nearly every day
Feeling nervous, anxious or on edge	0	1	2	3
Not being able to stop or control worrying	0	1	2	3
Worrying too much about different things	0	1	2	3
Trouble relaxing	0	1	2	3
Feeling afraid, as if something awful might happen	0	1	2	3

What your total score means Your total score is a guide to how severe your anxiety disorder may be: •0 to 4 = mild anxiety •5 to 9 = moderate anxiety •10 to 14 = moderately severe anxiety •15 to 21 = severe anxiety If your score is 10 or higher, or if you feel that anxiety is affecting your daily life, call your doctor

HELPING OTHERS

It is often said that charity begins at home, and helping others is one of the most important ways to make the world a better place. To be able to truly help those in need, we must first recognize that there is a problem. Whether it's poverty, homelessness, or any other social issue, it's crucial to understand the root of the problem before we can move forward and provide assistance. This blog post will discuss the importance of recognizing that there is a problem and why it should be the first step to making a difference.

ACKNOWLEDGING THAT THERE IS A PROBLEM

Making the world a better place can seem like a daunting task. But if we start by recognizing the problems that exist and then take steps to help address them, we can have a real and lasting impact. It all starts with acknowledging that there is a problem.
It's easy to think that our own lives are the only ones that matter, and that problems in other parts of the world don't affect us. But when we come to understand the interconnectedness of our global community, we can recognize the importance of making a difference. We can see how helping others can actually make the world a better place for everyone.
The next step is to figure out how to make a positive impact. This could be as simple as volunteering at a local soup kitchen or donating money to a charity. It could also mean advocating for policy change or lending your voice to an important cause. No matter what you choose to do, it's important to realize that small efforts can have a big effect.
Finally, it's important to stay committed and take action. Every day brings new opportunities to make the world a better place, so look for ways to contribute and do your part. It may not seem like much at first, but if we all work together, we can create real and lasting change.

TAKING ACTION

We all have a part to play in making the world a better place. It begins with recognizing that there is a problem, and then following up with actions that will help make a positive difference. To help us all make a bigger impact, here are some practical ideas on how to make the world a better place:

1. Practice Kindness – A little kindness can go a long way in making the world a better place. Showing compassion, understanding, and empathy can help improve our relationships with others and create a more harmonious atmosphere.

2. Spread Positivity – Instead of engaging in negative conversations, try to focus on being optimistic and uplifting those around you. Encourage others to think positively about the world, and share your own ideas for how we can make it better.

3. Volunteer – If you have the time and resources, volunteering can be a great way to help those in need and make a positive contribution to society. Whether it's helping out at a soup kitchen or helping the elders, providing free services at a music charity event or an animal shelter, there are plenty of ways to get involved.

4. Support Local Causes – Supporting local causes in your area can help make a big difference. Take some time to research local initiatives in your community and see what you can do to get involved.

5. Donate – If you can afford it, donating money to causes that support social justice, environmental conservation, and poverty alleviation can make a huge difference. Even small donations can help provide much-needed funds for those who are struggling.